Character Voices

A workbook for audiobook narration

Renee Conoulty

Introduction

In Narrated by the Author: How to Produce an Audiobook on a Budget, I went through all the technical steps to recording, editing, mastering and distributing an audiobook. But that's not all there is to creating an audiobook. Before you even switch on your microphone, you have to decide how your characters will sound.

If you have voice acting skills, fabulous. You can use this workbook to make additional notes on how each character will sound. If your voice acting skills are more like mine (you play with different voices when you read to your kids but they all sound a bit over the top, you keep mixing up which character had the squeaky voice and your kids laugh at you instead of with you) then you can use this workbook to choose simple variations and keep track of who sounds like what.

There are several ways you can use this book. As an author, you could use it during the writing process to get to know your characters better. As a narrator, you could use it during the preparation phase. You could use a separate copy of this book for each audiobook you narrate or take notes on several stories in the one volume. You could make notes on every single character from the book you plan to narrate, just the main ones or only the ones that come up less frequently. After a couple of practice runs, you'll work out which process works best for you. There's room for eight projects and 200 character voice descriptions in this book.

When characters are written, they have different speech patterns and vocabulary to give them individual voices on the page. When narrating, there are many aspects to spoken voice that can bring your characters to life and help them sound different from each other. Here are some simple ones to start with.

Pitch – use a higher pitch for a woman or child, a lower pitch for a man. Tempo – have characters speak at different speeds, not too fast or slow though otherwise, it can be difficult for the listener to understand. Cadence – you may have a character who speaks in a monotone, one with a melodic voice, or one whose voice goes up at the end of each sentence like it's a question. Accents and speech impediments are another way to give characters individuality but subtlety is the key. I shudder when I hear someone butcher the Australian accent (which is pretty much every non-native speaker who attempts it) and you don't want to sound like you're poking fun at people with speech impediments. The posture you hold while speaking can change the sound of your voice so standing tall for a confident character or slouching for an unmotivated character may give depth to your performance.

Each individual character may also sound different throughout the book, depending on what is happening at the time. Adding emotion to the voices can really help bring the story to life. You could do this by softening your voice during a proclamation of love or speeding up your voice during an action scene. Imagine how you would sound if you were feeling that emotion.

Pre-reading and making notes on the manuscript can make it much easier to narrate. Allocating a colour to each frequent character and highlighting their respective dialogue passages is a great way to keep track of who is saying what. You could underline words that need emphasis. You could change the font colour of words that you have difficulty pronouncing and change them in the document to the phonetic spelling.

You could print the document to do this, but this would cost more and turning paper pages will make additional noise that you will need to edit from the audio file. You could use a word processing program like Word to highlight different character's dialogue in different colours. It's easier to do this on a computer, but because of the background noise the computer fan makes, it's better to read the document on a smartphone or tablet. It's much easier to do a little preparation than to retake the scenes.

Character Voice Inspiration

If you like voice acting, you could base your character voices off celebrities, actors or people you know. You could try method acting and imagine that you are the character you're voicing. You could take inspiration from these descriptive words.

- Breathy
- Bright
- Brittle
- Chesty
- Cold
- Croaky
- Crying
- Drawl
- Fast
- Flat
- Flirty
- Grating
- Gravelly
- Gruff
- Hard
- High pitched
- Husky
- Laughing
- Loud
- Low pitched
- Lyrical
- Mid pitched
- Mumbling
- Nasal
- Panting

- Quiet
- Shrill
- Slow
- Soft
- Strong
- Thin
- Thready
- Throaty
- Tight
- Warm

- Afraid
- Angry
- Annoyed
- Aroused
- Ashamed
- Awkward
- Bored
- Bubbly
- Calm
- Courageous
- Depressed
- Disgusted
- Distracted
- Embarrassed
- Enthusiastic
- Envious
- Excited
- Exhausted
- Happy
- Indignant
- Jaded
- Love
- Nervous
- Pity
- Sad
- Sarcastic
- Surprised

- Accent
- Adult
- Child
- Cruel
- Egotistical
- Elderly
- Friendly
- Imposing
- Kind
- Lisp
- Man
- Meek
- Monotonous
- Nerdy
- Plummy
- Quirky
- Shy
- Sinister
- Snobby
- Stutter
- Sweet
- Teenager
- Woman

Audiobook Technical Requirements

• Each chapter, credits, introduction etc must be uploaded as a separate file.

• Opening and closing credits must be included.

• All audio must be human narrated and provided in FLAC or mp3 files.

• Each file should have a bit rate of 192 kbps and sample rate of 44.1 kHz.

• Each individual file must have between 0.5-1 second of room tone at the start and 1-5 seconds of room tone at the end.

• RMS for each file must be between -23dB and -18 dB, with a peak below -3 dB and floor bellow -60 dB.

• No copyright materials or extraneous sounds.

If you don't know what all this means, grab yourself a copy of Narrated by the Author: How to Produce an Audiobook on a Budget.

http://books2read.com/narrated

Preferred recording settings

Book title _____

Recording location _____

Sample/project rate – 44.1 kHz/44100 Hz

Microphone name _____

Stereo ⚪   Mono ⚪

Microphone volume _____

File path _____

_____

_____

Notes _____

_____

_____

_____

_____

_____

Preferred recording settings

Book title _____

Recording location _____

Sample/project rate – 44.1 kHz/44100 Hz

Microphone name _____

Stereo ◯   Mono ◯

Microphone volume _____

File path _____

_____

_____

Notes _____

_____

_____

_____

_____

_____

Preferred recording settings

Book title _____

Recording location _____

Sample/project rate – 44.1 kHz/44100 Hz

Microphone name _____

Stereo ◯   Mono ◯

Microphone volume _____

File path _____

_____

_____

Notes _____

_____

_____

_____

_____

_____

Preferred recording settings

Book title _____

Recording location _____

Sample/project rate – 44.1 kHz/44100 Hz

Microphone name _____

Stereo ◯   Mono ◯

Microphone volume _____

File path _____

_____

_____

Notes _____

_____

_____

_____

_____

_____

Preferred recording settings

Book title _____

Recording location _____

Sample/project rate – 44.1 kHz/44100 Hz

Microphone name _____

Stereo ◯   Mono ◯

Microphone volume _____

File path _____

_____

_____

Notes _____

_____

_____

_____

_____

_____

Preferred recording settings

Book title _____

Recording location _____

Sample/project rate – 44.1 kHz/44100 Hz

Microphone name _____

Stereo ◯   Mono ◯

Microphone volume _____

File path _____

_____

_____

Notes _____

_____

_____

_____

_____

_____

Preferred recording settings

Book title _____

Recording location _____

Sample/project rate – 44.1 kHz/44100 Hz

Microphone name _____

Stereo ◯   Mono ◯

Microphone volume _____

File path _____

_____

_____

Notes _____

_____

_____

_____

_____

_____

Preferred recording settings

Book title _____

Recording location _____

Sample/project rate – 44.1 kHz/44100 Hz

Microphone name _____

Stereo ○   Mono ○

Microphone volume _____

File path _____

_____

_____

Notes _____

_____

_____

_____

_____

_____

_____

Credits

Opening credits –

[Title _____]

Written by [author _____]

Narrated by [narrator _____]

Closing credits –

This has been [title _____]

Written by [author _____]

Narrated by [narrator _____]

Copyright [year book published _____]

by [author _____]

Production copyright

[year recorded _____]

by [narrator _____]

Credits

Opening credits –

[Title _____]

Written by [author _____]

Narrated by [narrator _____]

Closing credits –

 This has been [title _____]

Written by [author _____]

Narrated by [narrator _____]

Copyright [year book published _____]

by [author _____]

Production copyright

[year recorded _____]

by [narrator _____]

Credits

Opening credits –

[Title _____]

Written by [author _____]

Narrated by [narrator _____]

Closing credits –

This has been [title _____]

Written by [author _____]

Narrated by [narrator _____]

Copyright [year book published _____]

by [author _____]

Production copyright

[year recorded _____]

by [narrator _____]

Credits

Opening credits –

[Title _____]

Written by [author _____]

Narrated by [narrator _____]

Closing credits –

This has been [title _____]

Written by [author _____]

Narrated by [narrator _____]

Copyright [year book published _____]

by [author _____]

Production copyright

[year recorded _____]

by [narrator _____]

Credits

Opening credits –

[Title _____]

Written by [author _____]

Narrated by [narrator _____]

Closing credits –

This has been [title _____]

Written by [author _____]

Narrated by [narrator _____]

Copyright [year book published _____]

by [author _____]

Production copyright

[year recorded _____]

by [narrator _____]

Credits

Opening credits –

[Title _____]

Written by [author _____]

Narrated by [narrator _____]

Closing credits –

This has been [title _____]

Written by [author _____]

Narrated by [narrator _____]

Copyright [year book published _____]

by [author _____]

Production copyright

[year recorded _____]

by [narrator _____]

Credits

Opening credits –

[Title _____]

Written by [author _____]

Narrated by [narrator _____]

Closing credits –

This has been [title _____]

Written by [author _____]

Narrated by [narrator _____]

Copyright [year book published _____]

by [author _____]

Production copyright

[year recorded _____]

by [narrator _____]

Credits

Opening credits –

[Title _____]

Written by [author _____]

Narrated by [narrator _____]

Closing credits –

This has been [title _____]

Written by [author _____]

Narrated by [narrator _____]

Copyright [year book published _____]

by [author _____]

Production copyright

[year recorded _____]

by [narrator _____]

Character name _____

Colour code _____

Nationality/Accent _____

Age – child ◯ teen ◯ adult ◯ elderly ◯

Gender – male ♂ female ♀ other ◯

Tempo – slow ◯ regular ◯ fast ◯

Pitch – low ◯ regular ◯ high ◯

Personality traits _____

_____

Character quirks _____

Other voice description _____

_____

Notes _____

_____

_____

Book title _____

Character name _____

Colour code _____

Nationality/Accent _____

Age – child ◯ teen ◯ adult ◯ elderly ◯

Gender – male ♂ female ♀ other ◯

Tempo – slow ◯ regular ◯ fast ◯

Pitch – low ◯ regular ◯ high ◯

Personality traits _____

_____

Character quirks _____

Other voice description _____

_____

Notes _____

_____

_____

Book title _____

Character name _____

Colour code _____

Nationality/Accent _____

Age – child◯ teen◯ adult◯ elderly◯

Gender – male ♂ female ♀ other ◯

Tempo – slow ◯ regular ◯ fast◯

Pitch – low◯ regular◯ high◯

Personality traits _____

_____

Character quirks _____

Other voice description _____

_____

Notes _____

_____

_____

Book title _____

Character name _____

Colour code _____

Nationality/Accent _____

Age – child ◯ teen ◯ adult ◯ elderly ◯

Gender – male ♂ female ♀ other ◯

Tempo – slow ◯ regular ◯ fast ◯

Pitch – low ◯ regular ◯ high ◯

Personality traits _____

_____

Character quirks _____

Other voice description _____

_____

Notes _____

_____

_____

Book title _____

Character name _____

Colour code _____

Nationality/Accent _____

Age – child ◯ teen ◯ adult ◯ elderly ◯

Gender – male ♂ female ♀ other ◯

Tempo – slow ◯ regular ◯ fast ◯

Pitch – low ◯ regular ◯ high ◯

Personality traits _____

_____

Character quirks _____

Other voice description _____

_____

Notes _____

_____

_____

Book title _____

Character name _____

Colour code _____

Nationality/Accent _____

Age – child ◯ teen ◯ adult ◯ elderly ◯

Gender – male ♂ female ♀ other ◯

Tempo – slow ◯ regular ◯ fast ◯

Pitch – low ◯ regular ◯ high ◯

Personality traits _____

_____

Character quirks _____

Other voice description _____

_____

Notes _____

_____

_____

Book title _____

Character name _____

Colour code _____

Nationality/Accent _____

Age – child◯ teen◯ adult◯ elderly◯

Gender – male ♂ female ♀ other ◯

Tempo – slow ◯ regular ◯ fast◯

Pitch – low◯ regular ◯ high ◯

Personality traits _____

_____

Character quirks _____

Other voice description _____

_____

Notes _____

_____

_____

Book title _____

Character name _____

Colour code _____

Nationality/Accent _____

Age – child ◯ teen ◯ adult ◯ elderly ◯

Gender – male ♂ female ♀ other ◯

Tempo – slow ◯ regular ◯ fast ◯

Pitch – low ◯ regular ◯ high ◯

Personality traits _____

_____

Character quirks _____

Other voice description _____

_____

Notes _____

_____

_____

Book title _____

Character name _____

Colour code _____

Nationality/Accent _____

Age – child◯ teen ◯ adult ◯ elderly◯

Gender – male ♂ female ♀ other ◯

Tempo – slow ◯ regular ◯ fast◯

Pitch – low◯ regular◯ high◯

Personality traits _____

_____

Character quirks _____

Other voice description _____

_____

Notes _____

_____

_____

Book title _____

Character name _____

Colour code _____

Nationality/Accent _____

Age – child ◯ teen ◯ adult ◯ elderly ◯

Gender – male ♂ female ♀ other ◯

Tempo – slow ◯ regular ◯ fast ◯

Pitch – low ◯ regular ◯ high ◯

Personality traits _____

_____

Character quirks _____

Other voice description _____

_____

Notes _____

_____

_____

Book title _____

Character name _____

Colour code _____

Nationality/Accent _____

Age – child ◯ teen ◯ adult ◯ elderly ◯

Gender – male ♂ female ♀ other ◯

Tempo – slow ◯ regular ◯ fast ◯

Pitch – low ◯ regular ◯ high ◯

Personality traits _____

_____

Character quirks _____

Other voice description _____

_____

Notes _____

_____

_____

Book title _____

Character name _____

Colour code _____

Nationality/Accent _____

Age – child ⃝ teen ⃝ adult ⃝ elderly ⃝

Gender – male ♂ female ♀ other ⃝

Tempo – slow ⃝ regular ⃝ fast ⃝

Pitch – low ⃝ regular ⃝ high ⃝

Personality traits _____

_____

Character quirks _____

Other voice description _____

_____

Notes _____

_____

_____

Book title _____

Character name _____

Colour code _____

Nationality/Accent _____

Age – child ◯　teen ◯　adult ◯　elderly ◯

Gender – male ♂　female ♀　other ◯

Tempo – slow ◯　regular ◯　fast ◯

Pitch – 　low ◯　regular ◯　high ◯

Personality traits _____

_____

Character quirks _____

Other voice description _____

_____

Notes _____

_____

_____

Book title _____

Character name _____

Colour code _____

Nationality/Accent _____

Age – child ◯ teen ◯ adult ◯ elderly ◯

Gender – male ♂ female ♀ other ◯

Tempo – slow ◯ regular ◯ fast ◯

Pitch – low ◯ regular ◯ high ◯

Personality traits _____

_____

Character quirks _____

Other voice description _____

_____

Notes _____

_____

_____

Book title _____

Character name _____

Colour code _____

Nationality/Accent _____

Age – child ◯ teen ◯ adult ◯ elderly ◯

Gender – male ♂ female ♀ other ◯

Tempo – slow ◯ regular ◯ fast ◯

Pitch – low ◯ regular ◯ high ◯

Personality traits _____

_____

Character quirks _____

Other voice description _____

_____

Notes _____

_____

_____

Book title _____

Character name _____

Colour code _____

Nationality/Accent _____

Age – child◯ teen◯ adult◯ elderly◯

Gender – male ♂ female ♀ other ◯

Tempo – slow◯ regular◯ fast◯

Pitch – low◯ regular◯ high◯

Personality traits _____

_____

Character quirks _____

Other voice description _____

_____

Notes _____

_____

_____

Book title _____

Character name _____

Colour code _____

Nationality/Accent _____

Age – child ◯ teen ◯ adult ◯ elderly ◯

Gender – male ♂ female ♀ other ◯

Tempo – slow ◯ regular ◯ fast ◯

Pitch – low ◯ regular ◯ high ◯

Personality traits _____

_____

Character quirks _____

Other voice description _____

_____

Notes _____

_____

_____

Book title _____

Character name _____

Colour code _____

Nationality/Accent _____

Age – child ◯ teen ◯ adult ◯ elderly ◯

Gender – male ♂ female ♀ other ◯

Tempo – slow ◯ regular ◯ fast ◯

Pitch – low ◯ regular ◯ high ◯

Personality traits _____

_____

Character quirks _____

Other voice description _____

_____

Notes _____

_____

_____

Book title _____

Character name _____

Colour code _____

Nationality/Accent _____

Age – child ⭕ teen ⭕ adult ⭕ elderly ⭕

Gender – male ♂ female ♀ other ⭕

Tempo – slow ⭕ regular ⭕ fast ⭕

Pitch – low ⭕ regular ⭕ high ⭕

Personality traits _____

_____

Character quirks _____

Other voice description _____

_____

Notes _____

_____

_____

Book title _____

Character name _____

Colour code _____

Nationality/Accent _____

Age – child ◯ teen ◯ adult ◯ elderly ◯

Gender – male ♂ female ♀ other ◯

Tempo – slow ◯ regular ◯ fast ◯

Pitch – low ◯ regular ◯ high ◯

Personality traits _____

_____

Character quirks _____

Other voice description _____

_____

Notes _____

_____

_____

Book title _____

Character name _____

Colour code _____

Nationality/Accent _____

Age – child ◯ teen ◯ adult ◯ elderly ◯

Gender – male ♂ female ♀ other ◯

Tempo – slow ◯ regular ◯ fast ◯

Pitch – low ◯ regular ◯ high ◯

Personality traits _____

_____

Character quirks _____

Other voice description _____

_____

Notes _____

_____

_____

Book title _____

Character name _____

Colour code _____

Nationality/Accent _____

Age – child ◯ teen ◯ adult ◯ elderly ◯

Gender – male ♂ female ♀ other ◯

Tempo – slow ◯ regular ◯ fast ◯

Pitch – low ◯ regular ◯ high ◯

Personality traits _____

_____

Character quirks _____

Other voice description _____

_____

Notes _____

_____

_____

Book title _____

Character name _____

Colour code _____

Nationality/Accent _____

Age – child ○ teen ○ adult ○ elderly ○

Gender – male ♂ female ♀ other ○

Tempo – slow ○ regular ○ fast ○

Pitch – low ○ regular ○ high ○

Personality traits _____

_____

Character quirks _____

Other voice description _____

_____

Notes _____

_____

_____

Book title _____

Character name _____

Colour code _____

Nationality/Accent _____

Age – child ◯ teen ◯ adult ◯ elderly ◯

Gender – male ♂ female ♀ other ◯

Tempo – slow ◯ regular ◯ fast ◯

Pitch – low ◯ regular ◯ high ◯

Personality traits _____

_____

Character quirks _____

Other voice description _____

_____

Notes _____

_____

_____

Book title _____

Character name _____

Colour code _____

Nationality/Accent _____

Age – child ○ teen ○ adult ○ elderly ○

Gender – male ♂ female ♀ other ○

Tempo – slow ○ regular ○ fast ○

Pitch – low ○ regular ○ high ○

Personality traits _____

_____

Character quirks _____

Other voice description _____

_____

Notes _____

_____

_____

Book title _____

Character name _____

Colour code _____

Nationality/Accent _____

Age – child ◯ teen ◯ adult ◯ elderly ◯

Gender – male ♂ female ♀ other ◯

Tempo – slow ◯ regular ◯ fast ◯

Pitch – low ◯ regular ◯ high ◯

Personality traits _____

_____

Character quirks _____

Other voice description _____

_____

Notes _____

_____

_____

Book title _____

Character name _____

Colour code _____

Nationality/Accent _____

Age – child ⃝ teen ⃝ adult ⃝ elderly ⃝

Gender – male ♂ female ♀ other ⃝

Tempo – slow ⃝ regular ⃝ fast ⃝

Pitch – low ⃝ regular ⃝ high ⃝

Personality traits _____

_____

Character quirks _____

Other voice description _____

_____

Notes _____

_____

_____

Book title _____

Character name _____

Colour code _____

Nationality/Accent _____

Age – child ◯ teen ◯ adult ◯ elderly ◯

Gender – male ♂ female ♀ other ◯

Tempo – slow ◯ regular ◯ fast ◯

Pitch – low ◯ regular ◯ high ◯

Personality traits _____

_____

Character quirks _____

Other voice description _____

_____

Notes _____

_____

_____

Book title _____

Character name _____

Colour code _____

Nationality/Accent _____

Age – child◯ teen◯ adult ◯ elderly◯

Gender – male ♂ female ♀ other ◯

Tempo – slow ◯ regular ◯ fast◯

Pitch – low◯ regular ◯ high◯

Personality traits _____

_____

Character quirks _____

Other voice description _____

_____

Notes _____

_____

_____

Book title _____

Character name _____

Colour code _____

Nationality/Accent _____

Age – child ◯ teen ◯ adult ◯ elderly ◯

Gender – male ♂ female ♀ other ◯

Tempo – slow ◯ regular ◯ fast ◯

Pitch – low ◯ regular ◯ high ◯

Personality traits _____

_____

Character quirks _____

Other voice description _____

_____

Notes _____

_____

_____

Book title _____

Character name _____

Colour code _____

Nationality/Accent _____

Age – child ◯ teen ◯ adult ◯ elderly ◯

Gender – male ♂ female ♀ other ◯

Tempo – slow ◯ regular ◯ fast ◯

Pitch – low ◯ regular ◯ high ◯

Personality traits _____

_____

Character quirks _____

Other voice description _____

_____

Notes _____

_____

_____

Book title _____

Character name _____

Colour code _____

Nationality/Accent _____

Age – child ◯ teen ◯ adult ◯ elderly ◯

Gender – male ♂ female ♀ other ◯

Tempo – slow ◯ regular ◯ fast ◯

Pitch – low ◯ regular ◯ high ◯

Personality traits _____

_____

Character quirks _____

Other voice description _____

_____

Notes _____

_____

_____

Book title _____

Character name _____

Colour code _____

Nationality/Accent _____

Age – child ◯ teen ◯ adult ◯ elderly ◯

Gender – male ♂ female ♀ other ◯

Tempo – slow ◯ regular ◯ fast ◯

Pitch – low ◯ regular ◯ high ◯

Personality traits _____

_____

Character quirks _____

Other voice description _____

_____

Notes _____

_____

_____

Book title _____

Character name _____

Colour code _____

Nationality/Accent _____

Age – child ◯ teen ◯ adult ◯ elderly ◯

Gender – male ♂ female ♀ other ◯

Tempo – slow ◯ regular ◯ fast ◯

Pitch – low ◯ regular ◯ high ◯

Personality traits _____

_____

Character quirks _____

Other voice description _____

_____

Notes _____

_____

_____

Book title _____

Character name _____

Colour code _____

Nationality/Accent _____

Age – child ◯ teen ◯ adult ◯ elderly ◯

Gender – male ♂ female ♀ other ◯

Tempo – slow ◯ regular ◯ fast ◯

Pitch – low ◯ regular ◯ high ◯

Personality traits _____

_____

Character quirks _____

Other voice description _____

_____

Notes _____

_____

_____

Book title _____

Character name _____

Colour code _____

Nationality/Accent _____

Age – child ◯ teen ◯ adult ◯ elderly ◯

Gender – male ♂ female ♀ other ◯

Tempo – slow ◯ regular ◯ fast ◯

Pitch – low ◯ regular ◯ high ◯

Personality traits _____

_____

Character quirks _____

Other voice description _____

_____

Notes _____

_____

_____

Book title _____

Character name _____

Colour code _____

Nationality/Accent _____

Age – child ⬭ teen ⬭ adult ⬭ elderly ⬭

Gender – male ♂ female ♀ other ⬭

Tempo – slow ⬭ regular ⬭ fast ⬭

Pitch – low ⬭ regular ⬭ high ⬭

Personality traits _____

_____

Character quirks _____

Other voice description _____

_____

Notes _____

_____

_____

Book title _____

Character name _____

Colour code _____

Nationality/Accent _____

Age – child ◯ teen ◯ adult ◯ elderly ◯

Gender – male ♂ female ♀ other ◯

Tempo – slow ◯ regular ◯ fast ◯

Pitch – low ◯ regular ◯ high ◯

Personality traits _____

_____

Character quirks _____

Other voice description _____

_____

Notes _____

_____

_____

Book title _____

Character name _____

Colour code _____

Nationality/Accent _____

Age – child ◯ teen ◯ adult ◯ elderly ◯

Gender – male ♂ female ♀ other ◯

Tempo – slow ◯ regular ◯ fast ◯

Pitch – low ◯ regular ◯ high ◯

Personality traits _____

_____

Character quirks _____

Other voice description _____

_____

Notes _____

_____

_____

Book title _____

Character name _____

Colour code _____

Nationality/Accent _____

Age – child ◯ teen ◯ adult ◯ elderly ◯

Gender – male ♂ female ♀ other ◯

Tempo – slow ◯ regular ◯ fast ◯

Pitch – low ◯ regular ◯ high ◯

Personality traits _____

_____

Character quirks _____

Other voice description _____

_____

Notes _____

_____

_____

Book title _____

Character name _____

Colour code _____

Nationality/Accent _____

Age – child ◯ teen ◯ adult ◯ elderly ◯

Gender – male ♂ female ♀ other ◯

Tempo – slow ◯ regular ◯ fast ◯

Pitch – low ◯ regular ◯ high ◯

Personality traits _____

_____

Character quirks _____

Other voice description _____

_____

Notes _____

_____

_____

Book title _____

Character name _____

Colour code _____

Nationality/Accent _____

Age – child ◯ teen ◯ adult ◯ elderly ◯

Gender – male ♂ female ♀ other ◯

Tempo – slow ◯ regular ◯ fast ◯

Pitch – low ◯ regular ◯ high ◯

Personality traits _____

_____

Character quirks _____

Other voice description _____

_____

Notes _____

_____

_____

Book title _____

Character name _____

Colour code _____

Nationality/Accent _____

Age – child ◯ teen ◯ adult ◯ elderly ◯

Gender – male ♂ female ♀ other ◯

Tempo – slow ◯ regular ◯ fast ◯

Pitch – low ◯ regular ◯ high ◯

Personality traits _____

_____

Character quirks _____

Other voice description _____

_____

Notes _____

_____

_____

Book title _____

Character name _____

Colour code _____

Nationality/Accent _____

Age – child ◯ teen ◯ adult ◯ elderly ◯

Gender – male ♂ female ♀ other ◯

Tempo – slow ◯ regular ◯ fast ◯

Pitch – low ◯ regular ◯ high ◯

Personality traits _____

_____

Character quirks _____

Other voice description _____

_____

Notes _____

_____

_____

Book title _____

Character name _____

Colour code _____

Nationality/Accent _____

Age – child◯ teen◯ adult◯ elderly◯

Gender – male ♂ female ♀ other ◯

Tempo – slow ◯ regular ◯ fast◯

Pitch – low◯ regular◯ high◯

Personality traits _____

_____

Character quirks _____

Other voice description _____

_____

Notes _____

_____

_____

Book title _____

Character name _____

Colour code _____

Nationality/Accent _____

Age – child ◯ teen ◯ adult ◯ elderly ◯

Gender – male ♂ female ♀ other ◯

Tempo – slow ◯ regular ◯ fast ◯

Pitch – low ◯ regular ◯ high ◯

Personality traits _____

_____

Character quirks _____

Other voice description _____

_____

Notes _____

_____

_____

Book title _____

Character name _____

Colour code _____

Nationality/Accent _____

Age – child ◯ teen ◯ adult ◯ elderly ◯

Gender – male ♂ female ♀ other ◯

Tempo – slow ◯ regular ◯ fast ◯

Pitch – low ◯ regular ◯ high ◯

Personality traits _____

_____

Character quirks _____

Other voice description _____

_____

Notes _____

_____

_____

Book title _____

Character name _____

Colour code _____

Nationality/Accent _____

Age – child ◯ teen ◯ adult ◯ elderly ◯

Gender – male ♂ female ♀ other ◯

Tempo – slow ◯ regular ◯ fast ◯

Pitch – low ◯ regular ◯ high ◯

Personality traits _____

_____

Character quirks _____

Other voice description _____

_____

Notes _____

_____

_____

Book title _____

Character name _____

Colour code _____

Nationality/Accent _____

Age – child ◯ teen ◯ adult ◯ elderly ◯

Gender – male ♂ female ♀ other ◯

Tempo – slow ◯ regular ◯ fast ◯

Pitch – low ◯ regular ◯ high ◯

Personality traits _____

_____

Character quirks _____

Other voice description _____

_____

Notes _____

_____

_____

Book title _____

Character name _____

Colour code _____

Nationality/Accent _____

Age – child ◯ teen ◯ adult ◯ elderly ◯

Gender – male ♂ female ♀ other ◯

Tempo – slow ◯ regular ◯ fast ◯

Pitch – low ◯ regular ◯ high ◯

Personality traits _____

_____

Character quirks _____

Other voice description _____

_____

Notes _____

_____

_____

Book title _____

Character name _____

Colour code _____

Nationality/Accent _____

Age – child ◯ teen ◯ adult ◯ elderly ◯

Gender – male ♂ female ♀ other ◯

Tempo – slow ◯ regular ◯ fast ◯

Pitch – low ◯ regular ◯ high ◯

Personality traits _____

_____

Character quirks _____

Other voice description _____

_____

Notes _____

_____

_____

Book title _____

Character name _____

Colour code _____

Nationality/Accent _____

Age – child ◯ teen ◯ adult ◯ elderly ◯

Gender – male ♂ female ♀ other ◯

Tempo – slow ◯ regular ◯ fast ◯

Pitch – low ◯ regular ◯ high ◯

Personality traits _____

_____

Character quirks _____

Other voice description _____

_____

Notes _____

_____

_____

Book title _____

Character name _____

Colour code _____

Nationality/Accent _____

Age – child ◯ teen ◯ adult ◯ elderly ◯

Gender – male ♂ female ♀ other ◯

Tempo – slow ◯ regular ◯ fast ◯

Pitch – low ◯ regular ◯ high ◯

Personality traits _____

_____

Character quirks _____

Other voice description _____

_____

Notes _____

_____

_____

Book title _____

Character name _____

Colour code _____

Nationality/Accent _____

Age – child ◯ teen ◯ adult ◯ elderly ◯

Gender – male ♂ female ♀ other ◯

Tempo – slow ◯ regular ◯ fast ◯

Pitch – low ◯ regular ◯ high ◯

Personality traits _____

_____

Character quirks _____

Other voice description _____

_____

Notes _____

_____

_____

Book title _____

Character name _____

Colour code _____

Nationality/Accent _____

Age – child◯ teen◯ adult ◯ elderly◯

Gender – male ♂ female ♀ other ◯

Tempo – slow ◯ regular ◯ fast◯

Pitch – low◯ regular ◯ high ◯

Personality traits _____

_____

Character quirks _____

Other voice description _____

_____

Notes _____

_____

_____

Book title _____

Character name _____

Colour code _____

Nationality/Accent _____

Age – child ○ teen ○ adult ○ elderly ○

Gender – male ♂ female ♀ other ○

Tempo – slow ○ regular ○ fast ○

Pitch – low ○ regular ○ high ○

Personality traits _____

_____

Character quirks _____

Other voice description _____

_____

Notes _____

_____

_____

Book title _____

Character name _____

Colour code _____

Nationality/Accent _____

Age – child ◯ teen ◯ adult ◯ elderly ◯

Gender – male ♂ female ♀ other ◯

Tempo – slow ◯ regular ◯ fast ◯

Pitch – low ◯ regular ◯ high ◯

Personality traits _____

_____

Character quirks _____

Other voice description _____

_____

Notes _____

_____

_____

Book title _____

Character name _____

Colour code _____

Nationality/Accent _____

Age – child ◯ teen ◯ adult ◯ elderly ◯

Gender – male ♂ female ♀ other ◯

Tempo – slow ◯ regular ◯ fast ◯

Pitch – low ◯ regular ◯ high ◯

Personality traits _____

_____

Character quirks _____

Other voice description _____

_____

Notes _____

_____

_____

Book title _____

Character name _____

Colour code _____

Nationality/Accent _____

Age – child ◯ teen ◯ adult ◯ elderly ◯

Gender – male ♂ female ♀ other ◯

Tempo – slow ◯ regular ◯ fast ◯

Pitch – low ◯ regular ◯ high ◯

Personality traits _____

_____

Character quirks _____

Other voice description _____

_____

Notes _____

_____

_____

Book title _____

Character name _____

Colour code _____

Nationality/Accent _____

Age – child ◯ teen ◯ adult ◯ elderly ◯

Gender – male ♂ female ♀ other ◯

Tempo – slow ◯ regular ◯ fast ◯

Pitch – low ◯ regular ◯ high ◯

Personality traits _____

_____

Character quirks _____

Other voice description _____

_____

Notes _____

_____

_____

Book title _____

Character name _____

Colour code _____

Nationality/Accent _____

Age – child◯ teen◯ adult◯ elderly◯

Gender – male ♂ female ♀ other ◯

Tempo – slow ◯ regular ◯ fast◯

Pitch – low◯ regular ◯ high◯

Personality traits _____

_____

Character quirks _____

Other voice description _____

_____

Notes _____

_____

_____

Book title _____

Character name _____

Colour code _____

Nationality/Accent _____

Age – child ◯ teen ◯ adult ◯ elderly ◯

Gender – male ♂ female ♀ other ◯

Tempo – slow ◯ regular ◯ fast ◯

Pitch – low ◯ regular ◯ high ◯

Personality traits _____

_____

Character quirks _____

Other voice description _____

_____

Notes _____

_____

_____

Book title _____

Character name _____

Colour code _____

Nationality/Accent _____

Age – child ◯ teen ◯ adult ◯ elderly ◯

Gender – male ♂ female ♀ other ◯

Tempo – slow ◯ regular ◯ fast ◯

Pitch – low ◯ regular ◯ high ◯

Personality traits _____

_____

Character quirks _____

Other voice description _____

_____

Notes _____

_____

_____

Book title _____

Character name _____

Colour code _____

Nationality/Accent _____

Age – child ○ teen ○ adult ○ elderly ○

Gender – male ♂ female ♀ other ○

Tempo – slow ○ regular ○ fast ○

Pitch – low ○ regular ○ high ○

Personality traits _____

_____

Character quirks _____

Other voice description _____

_____

Notes _____

_____

_____

Book title _____

Character name _____

Colour code _____

Nationality/Accent _____

Age – child ◯ teen ◯ adult ◯ elderly ◯

Gender – male ♂ female ♀ other ◯

Tempo – slow ◯ regular ◯ fast ◯

Pitch – low ◯ regular ◯ high ◯

Personality traits _____

_____

Character quirks _____

Other voice description _____

_____

Notes _____

_____

_____

Book title _____

Character name _____

Colour code _____

Nationality/Accent _____

Age – child ◯ teen ◯ adult ◯ elderly ◯

Gender – male ♂ female ♀ other ◯

Tempo – slow ◯ regular ◯ fast ◯

Pitch – low ◯ regular ◯ high ◯

Personality traits _____

_____

Character quirks _____

Other voice description _____

_____

Notes _____

_____

_____

Book title _____

Character name _____

Colour code _____

Nationality/Accent _____

Age – child ◯ teen ◯ adult ◯ elderly ◯

Gender – male ♂ female ♀ other ◯

Tempo – slow ◯ regular ◯ fast ◯

Pitch – low ◯ regular ◯ high ◯

Personality traits _____

_____

Character quirks _____

Other voice description _____

_____

Notes _____

_____

_____

Book title _____

Character name _____

Colour code _____

Nationality/Accent _____

Age – child ◯ teen ◯ adult ◯ elderly ◯

Gender – male ♂ female ♀ other ◯

Tempo – slow ◯ regular ◯ fast ◯

Pitch – low ◯ regular ◯ high ◯

Personality traits _____

_____

Character quirks _____

Other voice description _____

_____

Notes _____

_____

_____

Book title _____

Character name _____

Colour code _____

Nationality/Accent _____

Age – child◯ teen ◯ adult ◯ elderly◯

Gender – male ♂ female ♀ other ◯

Tempo – slow ◯ regular ◯ fast◯

Pitch – low◯ regular ◯ high ◯

Personality traits _____

_____

Character quirks _____

Other voice description _____

_____

Notes _____

_____

_____

Book title _____

Character name _____

Colour code _____

Nationality/Accent _____

Age – child ◯ teen ◯ adult ◯ elderly ◯

Gender – male ♂ female ♀ other ◯

Tempo – slow ◯ regular ◯ fast ◯

Pitch – low ◯ regular ◯ high ◯

Personality traits _____

_____

Character quirks _____

Other voice description _____

_____

Notes _____

_____

_____

Book title _____

Character name _____

Colour code _____

Nationality/Accent _____

Age – child ◯ teen ◯ adult ◯ elderly ◯

Gender – male ♂ female ♀ other ◯

Tempo – slow ◯ regular ◯ fast ◯

Pitch – low ◯ regular ◯ high ◯

Personality traits _____

_____

Character quirks _____

Other voice description _____

_____

Notes _____

_____

_____

Book title _____

Character name _____

Colour code _____

Nationality/Accent _____

Age – child ◯ teen ◯ adult ◯ elderly ◯

Gender – male ♂ female ♀ other ◯

Tempo – slow ◯ regular ◯ fast ◯

Pitch – low ◯ regular ◯ high ◯

Personality traits _____

_____

Character quirks _____

Other voice description _____

_____

Notes _____

_____

_____

Book title _____

Character name _____

Colour code _____

Nationality/Accent _____

Age – child ◯ teen ◯ adult ◯ elderly ◯

Gender – male ♂ female ♀ other ◯

Tempo – slow ◯ regular ◯ fast ◯

Pitch – low ◯ regular ◯ high ◯

Personality traits _____

_____

Character quirks _____

Other voice description _____

_____

Notes _____

_____

_____

Book title _____

Character name _____

Colour code _____

Nationality/Accent _____

Age – child ◯ teen ◯ adult ◯ elderly ◯

Gender – male ♂ female ♀ other ◯

Tempo – slow ◯ regular ◯ fast ◯

Pitch – low ◯ regular ◯ high ◯

Personality traits _____

_____

Character quirks _____

Other voice description _____

_____

Notes _____

_____

_____

Book title _____

Character name _____

Colour code _____

Nationality/Accent _____

Age – child ◯ teen ◯ adult ◯ elderly ◯

Gender – male ♂ female ♀ other ◯

Tempo – slow ◯ regular ◯ fast ◯

Pitch – low ◯ regular ◯ high ◯

Personality traits _____

_____

Character quirks _____

Other voice description _____

_____

Notes _____

_____

_____

Book title _____

Character name _____

Colour code _____

Nationality/Accent _____

Age – child ⃝ teen⃝ adult⃝ elderly⃝

Gender – male♂ female♀ other⃝

Tempo – slow⃝ regular ⃝ fast⃝

Pitch –   low⃝ regular⃝ high ⃝

Personality traits _____

_____

Character quirks _____

Other voice description _____

_____

Notes _____

_____

_____

Book title _____

Character name _____

Colour code _____

Nationality/Accent _____

Age – child ◯ teen ◯ adult ◯ elderly ◯

Gender – male ♂ female ♀ other ◯

Tempo – slow ◯ regular ◯ fast ◯

Pitch – low ◯ regular ◯ high ◯

Personality traits _____

_____

Character quirks _____

Other voice description _____

_____

Notes _____

_____

_____

Book title _____

Character name _____

Colour code _____

Nationality/Accent _____

Age – child ◯ teen ◯ adult ◯ elderly ◯

Gender – male ♂ female ♀ other ◯

Tempo – slow ◯ regular ◯ fast ◯

Pitch – low ◯ regular ◯ high ◯

Personality traits _____

_____

Character quirks _____

Other voice description _____

_____

Notes _____

_____

_____

Book title _____

Character name _____

Colour code _____

Nationality/Accent _____

Age – child ◯ teen ◯ adult ◯ elderly ◯

Gender – male ♂ female ♀ other ◯

Tempo – slow ◯ regular ◯ fast ◯

Pitch – low ◯ regular ◯ high ◯

Personality traits _____

_____

Character quirks _____

Other voice description _____

_____

Notes _____

_____

_____

Book title _____

Character name _____

Colour code _____

Nationality/Accent _____

Age – child ◯ teen ◯ adult ◯ elderly ◯

Gender – male ♂ female ♀ other ◯

Tempo – slow ◯ regular ◯ fast ◯

Pitch – low ◯ regular ◯ high ◯

Personality traits _____

_____

Character quirks _____

Other voice description _____

_____

Notes _____

_____

_____

Book title _____

Character name _____

Colour code _____

Nationality/Accent _____

Age – child ◯ teen ◯ adult ◯ elderly ◯

Gender – male ♂ female ♀ other ◯

Tempo – slow ◯ regular ◯ fast ◯

Pitch – low ◯ regular ◯ high ◯

Personality traits _____

_____

Character quirks _____

Other voice description _____

_____

Notes _____

_____

_____

Book title _____

Character name _____

Colour code _____

Nationality/Accent _____

Age – child ◯   teen ◯   adult ◯   elderly ◯

Gender – male ♂   female ♀   other ◯

Tempo – slow ◯   regular ◯   fast ◯

Pitch – low ◯   regular ◯   high ◯

Personality traits _____

_____

Character quirks _____

Other voice description _____

_____

Notes _____

_____

_____

Book title _____

Character name _____

Colour code _____

Nationality/Accent _____

Age – child ◯ teen ◯ adult ◯ elderly ◯

Gender – male ♂ female ♀ other ◯

Tempo – slow ◯ regular ◯ fast ◯

Pitch – low ◯ regular ◯ high ◯

Personality traits _____

_____

Character quirks _____

Other voice description _____

_____

Notes _____

_____

_____

Book title _____

Character name _____

Colour code _____

Nationality/Accent _____

Age – child ◯ teen ◯ adult ◯ elderly ◯

Gender – male ♂ female ♀ other ◯

Tempo – slow ◯ regular ◯ fast ◯

Pitch – low ◯ regular ◯ high ◯

Personality traits _____

_____

Character quirks _____

Other voice description _____

_____

Notes _____

_____

_____

Book title _____

Character name _____

Colour code _____

Nationality/Accent _____

Age – child ◯ teen◯ adult◯ elderly◯

Gender – male♂ female♀ other◯

Tempo – slow◯ regular◯ fast◯

Pitch – low◯ regular◯ high◯

Personality traits _____

_____

Character quirks _____

Other voice description _____

_____

Notes _____

_____

_____

Book title _____

Character name _____

Colour code _____

Nationality/Accent _____

Age – child ◯ teen ◯ adult ◯ elderly ◯

Gender – male ♂ female ♀ other ◯

Tempo – slow ◯ regular ◯ fast ◯

Pitch – low ◯ regular ◯ high ◯

Personality traits _____

_____

Character quirks _____

Other voice description _____

_____

Notes _____

_____

_____

Book title _____

Character name _____

Colour code _____

Nationality/Accent _____

Age – child ◯ teen ◯ adult ◯ elderly ◯

Gender – male ♂ female ♀ other ◯

Tempo – slow ◯ regular ◯ fast ◯

Pitch – low ◯ regular ◯ high ◯

Personality traits _____

_____

Character quirks _____

Other voice description _____

_____

Notes _____

_____

_____

Book title _____

Character name _____

Colour code _____

Nationality/Accent _____

Age – child ◯ teen ◯ adult ◯ elderly ◯

Gender – male ♂ female ♀ other ◯

Tempo – slow ◯ regular ◯ fast ◯

Pitch – low ◯ regular ◯ high ◯

Personality traits _____

_____

Character quirks _____

Other voice description _____

_____

Notes _____

_____

_____

Book title _____

Character name _____

Colour code _____

Nationality/Accent _____

Age – child ◯ teen ◯ adult ◯ elderly ◯

Gender – male ♂ female ♀ other ◯

Tempo – slow ◯ regular ◯ fast ◯

Pitch – low ◯ regular ◯ high ◯

Personality traits _____

_____

Character quirks _____

Other voice description _____

_____

Notes _____

_____

_____

Book title _____

Character name _____

Colour code _____

Nationality/Accent _____

Age – child ◯ teen◯ adult◯ elderly◯

Gender – male♂ female♀ other◯

Tempo – slow◯ regular◯ fast◯

Pitch – low◯ regular◯ high◯

Personality traits _____

_____

Character quirks _____

Other voice description _____

_____

Notes _____

_____

_____

Book title _____

Character name _____

Colour code _____

Nationality/Accent _____

Age – child ◯   teen ◯   adult ◯   elderly ◯

Gender – male ♂   female ♀   other ◯

Tempo – slow ◯   regular ◯   fast ◯

Pitch – low ◯   regular ◯   high ◯

Personality traits _____

_____

Character quirks _____

Other voice description _____

_____

Notes _____

_____

_____

Book title _____

Character name _____

Colour code _____

Nationality/Accent _____

Age – child ◯ teen ◯ adult ◯ elderly ◯

Gender – male ♂ female ♀ other ◯

Tempo – slow ◯ regular ◯ fast ◯

Pitch – low ◯ regular ◯ high ◯

Personality traits _____

_____

Character quirks _____

Other voice description _____

_____

Notes _____

_____

_____

Book title _____

Character name _____

Colour code _____

Nationality/Accent _____

Age – child ◯ teen ◯ adult ◯ elderly ◯

Gender – male ♂ female ♀ other ◯

Tempo – slow ◯ regular ◯ fast ◯

Pitch – low ◯ regular ◯ high ◯

Personality traits _____

_____

Character quirks _____

Other voice description _____

_____

Notes _____

_____

_____

Book title _____

Character name _____

Colour code _____

Nationality/Accent _____

Age – child ◯ teen ◯ adult ◯ elderly ◯

Gender – male ♂ female ♀ other ◯

Tempo – slow ◯ regular ◯ fast ◯

Pitch – low ◯ regular ◯ high ◯

Personality traits _____

_____

Character quirks _____

Other voice description _____

_____

Notes _____

_____

_____

Book title _____

Character name _____

Colour code _____

Nationality/Accent _____

Age – child ◯ teen ◯ adult ◯ elderly ◯

Gender – male ♂ female ♀ other ◯

Tempo – slow ◯ regular ◯ fast ◯

Pitch – low ◯ regular ◯ high ◯

Personality traits _____

_____

Character quirks _____

Other voice description _____

_____

Notes _____

_____

_____

Book title _____

Character name _____

Colour code _____

Nationality/Accent _____

Age – child ◯ teen ◯ adult ◯ elderly ◯

Gender – male ♂ female ♀ other ◯

Tempo – slow ◯ regular ◯ fast ◯

Pitch – low ◯ regular ◯ high ◯

Personality traits _____

_____

Character quirks _____

Other voice description _____

_____

Notes _____

_____

_____

Book title _____

Character name _____

Colour code _____

Nationality/Accent _____

Age – child ◯ teen ◯ adult ◯ elderly ◯

Gender – male ♂ female ♀ other ◯

Tempo – slow ◯ regular ◯ fast ◯

Pitch – low ◯ regular ◯ high ◯

Personality traits _____

_____

Character quirks _____

Other voice description _____

_____

Notes _____

_____

_____

Book title _____

Character name _____

Colour code _____

Nationality/Accent _____

Age – child ◯ teen ◯ adult ◯ elderly ◯

Gender – male ♂ female ♀ other ◯

Tempo – slow ◯ regular ◯ fast ◯

Pitch –   low ◯ regular ◯ high ◯

Personality traits _____

_____

Character quirks _____

Other voice description _____

_____

Notes _____

_____

_____

Book title _____

Character name _____

Colour code _____

Nationality/Accent _____

Age – child ◯ teen ◯ adult ◯ elderly ◯

Gender – male ♂ female ♀ other ◯

Tempo – slow ◯ regular ◯ fast ◯

Pitch – low ◯ regular ◯ high ◯

Personality traits _____

_____

Character quirks _____

Other voice description _____

_____

Notes _____

_____

_____

Book title _____

Character name _____

Colour code _____

Nationality/Accent _____

Age – child ◯ teen ◯ adult ◯ elderly ◯

Gender – male ♂ female ♀ other ◯

Tempo – slow ◯ regular ◯ fast ◯

Pitch – low ◯ regular ◯ high ◯

Personality traits _____

_____

Character quirks _____

Other voice description _____

_____

Notes _____

_____

_____

Book title _____

Character name _____

Colour code _____

Nationality/Accent _____

Age – child ◯ teen ◯ adult ◯ elderly ◯

Gender – male ♂ female ♀ other ◯

Tempo – slow ◯ regular ◯ fast ◯

Pitch – low ◯ regular ◯ high ◯

Personality traits _____

_____

Character quirks _____

Other voice description _____

_____

Notes _____

_____

_____

Book title _____

Character name _____

Colour code _____

Nationality/Accent _____

Age – child ◯　teen ◯　adult ◯　elderly ◯

Gender – male ♂　female ♀　other ◯

Tempo – slow ◯　regular ◯　fast ◯

Pitch – low ◯　regular ◯　high ◯

Personality traits _____

_____

Character quirks _____

Other voice description _____

_____

Notes _____

_____

_____

Book title _____

Character name _____

Colour code _____

Nationality/Accent _____

Age – child ◯　teen ◯　adult ◯　elderly ◯

Gender – male ♂　female ♀　other ◯

Tempo – slow ◯　regular ◯　fast ◯

Pitch – low ◯　regular ◯　high ◯

Personality traits _____

_____

Character quirks _____

Other voice description _____

_____

Notes _____

_____

_____

Book title _____

Character name _____

Colour code _____

Nationality/Accent _____

Age – child ◯ teen ◯ adult ◯ elderly ◯

Gender – male ♂ female ♀ other ◯

Tempo – slow ◯ regular ◯ fast ◯

Pitch – low ◯ regular ◯ high ◯

Personality traits _____

_____

Character quirks _____

Other voice description _____

_____

Notes _____

_____

_____

Book title _____

Character name _____

Colour code _____

Nationality/Accent _____

Age – child ◯ teen ◯ adult ◯ elderly ◯

Gender – male ♂ female ♀ other ◯

Tempo – slow ◯ regular ◯ fast ◯

Pitch – low ◯ regular ◯ high ◯

Personality traits _____

_____

Character quirks _____

Other voice description _____

_____

Notes _____

_____

_____

Book title _____

Character name _____

Colour code _____

Nationality/Accent _____

Age – child ◯ teen ◯ adult ◯ elderly ◯

Gender – male ♂ female ♀ other ◯

Tempo – slow ◯ regular ◯ fast ◯

Pitch – low ◯ regular ◯ high ◯

Personality traits _____

_____

Character quirks _____

Other voice description _____

_____

Notes _____

_____

_____

Book title _____

Character name _____

Colour code _____

Nationality/Accent _____

Age – child ◯ teen ◯ adult ◯ elderly ◯

Gender – male ♂ female ♀ other ◯

Tempo – slow ◯ regular ◯ fast ◯

Pitch – low ◯ regular ◯ high ◯

Personality traits _____

_____

Character quirks _____

Other voice description _____

_____

Notes _____

_____

_____

Book title _____

Character name _____

Colour code _____

Nationality/Accent _____

Age – child ◯ teen ◯ adult ◯ elderly ◯

Gender – male ♂ female ♀ other ◯

Tempo – slow ◯ regular ◯ fast ◯

Pitch – low ◯ regular ◯ high ◯

Personality traits _____

_____

Character quirks _____

Other voice description _____

_____

Notes _____

_____

_____

Book title _____

Character name _____

Colour code _____

Nationality/Accent _____

Age – child ◯   teen ◯   adult ◯   elderly ◯

Gender – male ♂   female ♀   other ◯

Tempo – slow ◯   regular ◯   fast ◯

Pitch – low ◯   regular ◯   high ◯

Personality traits _____

_____

Character quirks _____

Other voice description _____

_____

Notes _____

_____

_____

Book title _____

Character name _____

Colour code _____

Nationality/Accent _____

Age – child ◯ teen ◯ adult ◯ elderly ◯

Gender – male ♂ female ♀ other ◯

Tempo – slow ◯ regular ◯ fast ◯

Pitch – low ◯ regular ◯ high ◯

Personality traits _____

_____

Character quirks _____

Other voice description _____

_____

Notes _____

_____

_____

Book title _____

Character name _____

Colour code _____

Nationality/Accent _____

Age – child ◯ teen◯ adult◯ elderly◯

Gender – male♂ female♀ other◯

Tempo – slow◯ regular ◯ fast◯

Pitch –   low◯ regular◯ high ◯

Personality traits _____

_____

Character quirks _____

Other voice description _____

_____

Notes _____

_____

_____

Book title _____

Character name _____

Colour code _____

Nationality/Accent _____

Age – child ◯ teen ◯ adult ◯ elderly ◯

Gender – male ♂ female ♀ other ◯

Tempo – slow ◯ regular ◯ fast ◯

Pitch – low ◯ regular ◯ high ◯

Personality traits _____

_____

Character quirks _____

Other voice description _____

_____

Notes _____

_____

_____

Book title _____

Character name _____

Colour code _____

Nationality/Accent _____

Age – child ◯ teen ◯ adult ◯ elderly ◯

Gender – male ♂ female ♀ other ◯

Tempo – slow ◯ regular ◯ fast ◯

Pitch – low ◯ regular ◯ high ◯

Personality traits _____

_____

Character quirks _____

Other voice description _____

_____

Notes _____

_____

_____

Book title _____

Character name _____

Colour code _____

Nationality/Accent _____

Age – child ◯ teen ◯ adult ◯ elderly ◯

Gender – male ♂ female ♀ other ◯

Tempo – slow ◯ regular ◯ fast ◯

Pitch – low ◯ regular ◯ high ◯

Personality traits _____

_____

Character quirks _____

Other voice description _____

_____

Notes _____

_____

_____

Book title _____

Character name _____

Colour code _____

Nationality/Accent _____

Age – child ○ teen ○ adult ○ elderly ○

Gender – male ♂ female ♀ other ○

Tempo – slow ○ regular ○ fast ○

Pitch – low ○ regular ○ high ○

Personality traits _____

_____

Character quirks _____

Other voice description _____

_____

Notes _____

_____

_____

Book title _____

Character name _____

Colour code _____

Nationality/Accent _____

Age – child ◯ teen ◯ adult ◯ elderly ◯

Gender – male ♂ female ♀ other ◯

Tempo – slow ◯ regular ◯ fast ◯

Pitch – low ◯ regular ◯ high ◯

Personality traits _____

_____

Character quirks _____

Other voice description _____

_____

Notes _____

_____

_____

Book title _____

Character name _____

Colour code _____

Nationality/Accent _____

Age – child ◯ teen ◯ adult ◯ elderly ◯

Gender – male ♂ female ♀ other ◯

Tempo – slow ◯ regular ◯ fast ◯

Pitch – low ◯ regular ◯ high ◯

Personality traits _____

_____

Character quirks _____

Other voice description _____

_____

Notes _____

_____

_____

Book title _____

Character name _____

Colour code _____

Nationality/Accent _____

Age – child ◯   teen◯   adult◯   elderly◯

Gender – male♂   female♀   other◯

Tempo – slow◯   regular ◯   fast◯

Pitch –   low◯   regular◯   high ◯

Personality traits _____

_____

Character quirks _____

Other voice description _____

_____

Notes _____

_____

_____

Book title _____

Character name _____

Colour code _____

Nationality/Accent _____

Age – child ◯ teen ◯ adult ◯ elderly ◯

Gender – male ♂ female ♀ other ◯

Tempo – slow ◯ regular ◯ fast ◯

Pitch – low ◯ regular ◯ high ◯

Personality traits _____

_____

Character quirks _____

Other voice description _____

_____

Notes _____

_____

_____

Book title _____

Character name _____

Colour code _____

Nationality/Accent _____

Age – child ◯   teen◯   adult◯   elderly◯

Gender – male♂   female♀   other◯

Tempo – slow◯   regular ◯   fast◯

Pitch –   low◯   regular◯   high ◯

Personality traits _____

_____

Character quirks _____

Other voice description _____

_____

Notes _____

_____

_____

Book title _____

Character name _____

Colour code _____

Nationality/Accent _____

Age – child ◯ teen ◯ adult ◯ elderly ◯

Gender – male ♂ female ♀ other ◯

Tempo – slow ◯ regular ◯ fast ◯

Pitch – low ◯ regular ◯ high ◯

Personality traits _____

_____

Character quirks _____

Other voice description _____

_____

Notes _____

_____

_____

Book title _____

Character name _____

Colour code _____

Nationality/Accent _____

Age – child ◯ teen ◯ adult ◯ elderly ◯

Gender – male ♂ female ♀ other ◯

Tempo – slow ◯ regular ◯ fast ◯

Pitch – low ◯ regular ◯ high ◯

Personality traits _____

_____

Character quirks _____

Other voice description _____

_____

Notes _____

_____

_____

Book title _____

Character name _____

Colour code _____

Nationality/Accent _____

Age – child ◯ teen ◯ adult ◯ elderly ◯

Gender – male ♂ female ♀ other ◯

Tempo – slow ◯ regular ◯ fast ◯

Pitch – low ◯ regular ◯ high ◯

Personality traits _____

_____

Character quirks _____

Other voice description _____

_____

Notes _____

_____

_____

Book title _____

Character name _____

Colour code _____

Nationality/Accent _____

Age – child ◯ teen ◯ adult ◯ elderly ◯

Gender – male ♂ female ♀ other ◯

Tempo – slow ◯ regular ◯ fast ◯

Pitch – low ◯ regular ◯ high ◯

Personality traits _____

_____

Character quirks _____

Other voice description _____

_____

Notes _____

_____

_____

Book title _____

Character name _____

Colour code _____

Nationality/Accent _____

Age – child ◯ teen ◯ adult ◯ elderly ◯

Gender – male ♂ female ♀ other ◯

Tempo – slow ◯ regular ◯ fast ◯

Pitch – low ◯ regular ◯ high ◯

Personality traits _____

_____

Character quirks _____

Other voice description _____

_____

Notes _____

_____

_____

Book title _____

Character name _____

Colour code _____

Nationality/Accent _____

Age – child ◯ teen ◯ adult ◯ elderly ◯

Gender – male ♂ female ♀ other ◯

Tempo – slow ◯ regular ◯ fast ◯

Pitch – low ◯ regular ◯ high ◯

Personality traits _____

_____

Character quirks _____

Other voice description _____

_____

Notes _____

_____

_____

Book title _____

Character name _____

Colour code _____

Nationality/Accent _____

Age – child ◯ teen ◯ adult ◯ elderly ◯

Gender – male ♂ female ♀ other ◯

Tempo – slow ◯ regular ◯ fast ◯

Pitch – low ◯ regular ◯ high ◯

Personality traits _____

_____

Character quirks _____

Other voice description _____

_____

Notes _____

_____

_____

Book title _____

Character name _____

Colour code _____

Nationality/Accent _____

Age – child ◯ teen ◯ adult ◯ elderly ◯

Gender – male ♂ female ♀ other ◯

Tempo – slow ◯ regular ◯ fast ◯

Pitch – low ◯ regular ◯ high ◯

Personality traits _____

_____

Character quirks _____

Other voice description _____

_____

Notes _____

_____

_____

Book title _____

Character name _____

Colour code _____

Nationality/Accent _____

Age – child◯ teen◯ adult◯ elderly◯

Gender – male♂ female♀ other◯

Tempo – slow◯ regular◯ fast◯

Pitch – low◯ regular◯ high◯

Personality traits _____

_____

Character quirks _____

Other voice description _____

_____

Notes _____

_____

_____

Book title _____

Character name _____

Colour code _____

Nationality/Accent _____

Age – child ◯ teen ◯ adult ◯ elderly ◯

Gender – male ♂ female ♀ other ◯

Tempo – slow ◯ regular ◯ fast ◯

Pitch – low ◯ regular ◯ high ◯

Personality traits _____

_____

Character quirks _____

Other voice description _____

_____

Notes _____

_____

_____

Book title _____

Character name _____

Colour code _____

Nationality/Accent _____

Age – child ◯ teen ◯ adult ◯ elderly ◯

Gender – male ♂ female ♀ other ◯

Tempo – slow ◯ regular ◯ fast ◯

Pitch – low ◯ regular ◯ high ◯

Personality traits _____

_____

Character quirks _____

Other voice description _____

_____

Notes _____

_____

_____

Book title _____

Character name _____

Colour code _____

Nationality/Accent _____

Age – child ◯ teen ◯ adult ◯ elderly ◯

Gender – male ♂ female ♀ other ◯

Tempo – slow ◯ regular ◯ fast ◯

Pitch – low ◯ regular ◯ high ◯

Personality traits _____

_____

Character quirks _____

Other voice description _____

_____

Notes _____

_____

_____

Book title _____

Character name _____

Colour code _____

Nationality/Accent _____

Age – child ◯ teen ◯ adult ◯ elderly ◯

Gender – male ♂ female ♀ other ◯

Tempo – slow ◯ regular ◯ fast ◯

Pitch – low ◯ regular ◯ high ◯

Personality traits _____

_____

Character quirks _____

Other voice description _____

_____

Notes _____

_____

_____

Book title _____

Character name _____

Colour code _____

Nationality/Accent _____

Age – child ⃝ teen ⃝ adult ⃝ elderly ⃝

Gender – male ♂ female ♀ other ⃝

Tempo – slow ⃝ regular ⃝ fast ⃝

Pitch – low ⃝ regular ⃝ high ⃝

Personality traits _____

_____

Character quirks _____

Other voice description _____

_____

Notes _____

_____

_____

Book title _____

Character name _____

Colour code _____

Nationality/Accent _____

Age – child ◯ teen ◯ adult ◯ elderly ◯

Gender – male ♂ female ♀ other ◯

Tempo – slow ◯ regular ◯ fast ◯

Pitch – low ◯ regular ◯ high ◯

Personality traits _____

_____

Character quirks _____

Other voice description _____

_____

Notes _____

_____

_____

Book title _____

Character name _____

Colour code _____

Nationality/Accent _____

Age – child◯ teen◯ adult◯ elderly◯

Gender – male♂ female♀ other◯

Tempo – slow◯ regular◯ fast◯

Pitch – low◯ regular◯ high◯

Personality traits _____

_____

Character quirks _____

Other voice description _____

_____

Notes _____

_____

_____

Book title _____

Character name _____

Colour code _____

Nationality/Accent _____

Age – child ◯ teen ◯ adult ◯ elderly ◯

Gender – male ♂ female ♀ other ◯

Tempo – slow ◯ regular ◯ fast ◯

Pitch – low ◯ regular ◯ high ◯

Personality traits _____

_____

Character quirks _____

Other voice description _____

_____

Notes _____

_____

_____

Book title _____

Character name _____

Colour code _____

Nationality/Accent _____

Age – child ◯ teen ◯ adult ◯ elderly ◯

Gender – male ♂ female ♀ other ◯

Tempo – slow ◯ regular ◯ fast ◯

Pitch – low ◯ regular ◯ high ◯

Personality traits _____

_____

Character quirks _____

Other voice description _____

_____

Notes _____

_____

_____

Book title _____

Character name _____

Colour code _____

Nationality/Accent _____

Age – child ◯ teen ◯ adult ◯ elderly ◯

Gender – male ♂ female ♀ other ◯

Tempo – slow ◯ regular ◯ fast ◯

Pitch – low ◯ regular ◯ high ◯

Personality traits _____

_____

Character quirks _____

Other voice description _____

_____

Notes _____

_____

_____

Book title _____

Character name _____

Colour code _____

Nationality/Accent _____

Age – child ◯ teen ◯ adult ◯ elderly ◯

Gender – male ♂ female ♀ other ◯

Tempo – slow ◯ regular ◯ fast ◯

Pitch – low ◯ regular ◯ high ◯

Personality traits _____

_____

Character quirks _____

Other voice description _____

_____

Notes _____

_____

_____

Book title _____

Character name _____

Colour code _____

Nationality/Accent _____

Age – child ◯ teen ◯ adult ◯ elderly ◯

Gender – male ♂ female ♀ other ◯

Tempo – slow ◯ regular ◯ fast ◯

Pitch – low ◯ regular ◯ high ◯

Personality traits _____

_____

Character quirks _____

Other voice description _____

_____

Notes _____

_____

_____

Book title _____

Character name _____

Colour code _____

Nationality/Accent _____

Age – child ◯ teen ◯ adult ◯ elderly ◯

Gender – male ♂ female ♀ other ◯

Tempo – slow ◯ regular ◯ fast ◯

Pitch – low ◯ regular ◯ high ◯

Personality traits _____

_____

Character quirks _____

Other voice description _____

_____

Notes _____

_____

_____

Book title _____

Character name _____

Colour code _____

Nationality/Accent _____

Age – child ◯ teen ◯ adult ◯ elderly ◯

Gender – male ♂ female ♀ other ◯

Tempo – slow ◯ regular ◯ fast ◯

Pitch – low ◯ regular ◯ high ◯

Personality traits _____

_____

Character quirks _____

Other voice description _____

_____

Notes _____

_____

_____

Book title _____

Character name _____

Colour code _____

Nationality/Accent _____

Age – child ○ teen ○ adult ○ elderly ○

Gender – male ♂ female ♀ other ○

Tempo – slow ○ regular ○ fast ○

Pitch – low ○ regular ○ high ○

Personality traits _____

_____

Character quirks _____

Other voice description _____

_____

Notes _____

_____

_____

Book title _____

Character name _____

Colour code _____

Nationality/Accent _____

Age – child ◯ teen ◯ adult ◯ elderly ◯

Gender – male ♂ female ♀ other ◯

Tempo – slow ◯ regular ◯ fast ◯

Pitch – low ◯ regular ◯ high ◯

Personality traits _____

_____

Character quirks _____

Other voice description _____

_____

Notes _____

_____

_____

Book title _____

Character name _____

Colour code _____

Nationality/Accent _____

Age – child ◯ teen ◯ adult ◯ elderly ◯

Gender – male ♂ female ♀ other ◯

Tempo – slow ◯ regular ◯ fast ◯

Pitch – low ◯ regular ◯ high ◯

Personality traits _____

_____

Character quirks _____

Other voice description _____

_____

Notes _____

_____

_____

Book title _____

Character name _____

Colour code _____

Nationality/Accent _____

Age – child ⃝ teen ⃝ adult ⃝ elderly ⃝

Gender – male ♂ female ♀ other ⃝

Tempo – slow ⃝ regular ⃝ fast ⃝

Pitch – low ⃝ regular ⃝ high ⃝

Personality traits _____

_____

Character quirks _____

Other voice description _____

_____

Notes _____

_____

_____

Book title _____

Character name _____

Colour code _____

Nationality/Accent _____

Age – child ◯ teen ◯ adult ◯ elderly ◯

Gender – male ♂ female ♀ other ◯

Tempo – slow ◯ regular ◯ fast ◯

Pitch – low ◯ regular ◯ high ◯

Personality traits _____

_____

Character quirks _____

Other voice description _____

_____

Notes _____

_____

_____

Book title _____

Character name _____

Colour code _____

Nationality/Accent _____

Age – child ◯ teen ◯ adult ◯ elderly ◯

Gender – male ♂ female ♀ other ◯

Tempo – slow ◯ regular ◯ fast ◯

Pitch – low ◯ regular ◯ high ◯

Personality traits _____

_____

Character quirks _____

Other voice description _____

_____

Notes _____

_____

_____

Book title _____

Character name _____

Colour code _____

Nationality/Accent _____

Age – child ◯ teen ◯ adult ◯ elderly ◯

Gender – male ♂ female ♀ other ◯

Tempo – slow ◯ regular ◯ fast ◯

Pitch – low ◯ regular ◯ high ◯

Personality traits _____

_____

Character quirks _____

Other voice description _____

_____

Notes _____

_____

_____

Book title _____

Character name _____

Colour code _____

Nationality/Accent _____

Age – child ◯ teen ◯ adult ◯ elderly ◯

Gender – male ♂ female ♀ other ◯

Tempo – slow ◯ regular ◯ fast ◯

Pitch – low ◯ regular ◯ high ◯

Personality traits _____

_____

Character quirks _____

Other voice description _____

_____

Notes _____

_____

_____

Book title _____

Character name _____

Colour code _____

Nationality/Accent _____

Age – child ◯　teen ◯　adult ◯　elderly ◯

Gender – male ♂　female ♀　other ◯

Tempo – slow ◯　regular ◯　fast ◯

Pitch – 　low ◯　regular ◯　high ◯

Personality traits _____

_____

Character quirks _____

Other voice description _____

_____

Notes _____

_____

_____

Book title _____

Character name _____

Colour code _____

Nationality/Accent _____

Age – child ◯ teen ◯ adult ◯ elderly ◯

Gender – male ♂ female ♀ other ◯

Tempo – slow ◯ regular ◯ fast ◯

Pitch – low ◯ regular ◯ high ◯

Personality traits _____

_____

Character quirks _____

Other voice description _____

_____

Notes _____

_____

_____

Book title _____

Character name _____

Colour code _____

Nationality/Accent _____

Age – child ◯ teen ◯ adult ◯ elderly ◯

Gender – male ♂ female ♀ other ◯

Tempo – slow ◯ regular ◯ fast ◯

Pitch – low ◯ regular ◯ high ◯

Personality traits _____

_____

Character quirks _____

Other voice description _____

_____

Notes _____

_____

_____

Book title _____

Character name _____

Colour code _____

Nationality/Accent _____

Age – child ◯ teen◯ adult◯ elderly◯

Gender – male♂ female♀ other◯

Tempo – slow◯ regular◯ fast◯

Pitch – low◯ regular◯ high◯

Personality traits _____

_____

Character quirks _____

Other voice description _____

_____

Notes _____

_____

_____

Book title _____

Character name _____

Colour code _____

Nationality/Accent _____

Age – child ◯ teen ◯ adult ◯ elderly ◯

Gender – male ♂ female ♀ other ◯

Tempo – slow ◯ regular ◯ fast ◯

Pitch – low ◯ regular ◯ high ◯

Personality traits _____

_____

Character quirks _____

Other voice description _____

_____

Notes _____

_____

_____

Book title _____

Character name _____

Colour code _____

Nationality/Accent _____

Age – child ◯ teen ◯ adult ◯ elderly ◯

Gender – male ♂ female ♀ other ◯

Tempo – slow ◯ regular ◯ fast ◯

Pitch – low ◯ regular ◯ high ◯

Personality traits _____

_____

Character quirks _____

Other voice description _____

_____

Notes _____

_____

_____

Book title _____

Character name _____

Colour code _____

Nationality/Accent _____

Age – child ◯ teen ◯ adult ◯ elderly ◯

Gender – male ♂ female ♀ other ◯

Tempo – slow ◯ regular ◯ fast ◯

Pitch – low ◯ regular ◯ high ◯

Personality traits _____

_____

Character quirks _____

Other voice description _____

_____

Notes _____

_____

_____

Book title _____

Character name _____

Colour code _____

Nationality/Accent _____

Age – child ◯ teen ◯ adult ◯ elderly ◯

Gender – male ♂ female ♀ other ◯

Tempo – slow ◯ regular ◯ fast ◯

Pitch – low ◯ regular ◯ high ◯

Personality traits _____

_____

Character quirks _____

Other voice description _____

_____

Notes _____

_____

_____

Book title _____

Character name _____

Colour code _____

Nationality/Accent _____

Age – child ◯ teen ◯ adult ◯ elderly ◯

Gender – male ♂ female ♀ other ◯

Tempo – slow ◯ regular ◯ fast ◯

Pitch – low ◯ regular ◯ high ◯

Personality traits _____

_____

Character quirks _____

Other voice description _____

_____

Notes _____

_____

_____

Book title _____

Character name _____

Colour code _____

Nationality/Accent _____

Age – child ◯ teen ◯ adult ◯ elderly ◯

Gender – male ♂ female ♀ other ◯

Tempo – slow ◯ regular ◯ fast ◯

Pitch – low ◯ regular ◯ high ◯

Personality traits _____

_____

Character quirks _____

Other voice description _____

_____

Notes _____

_____

_____

Book title _____

Character name _____

Colour code _____

Nationality/Accent _____

Age – child ◯ teen ◯ adult ◯ elderly ◯

Gender – male ♂ female ♀ other ◯

Tempo – slow ◯ regular ◯ fast ◯

Pitch – low ◯ regular ◯ high ◯

Personality traits _____

_____

Character quirks _____

Other voice description _____

_____

Notes _____

_____

_____

Book title _____

Character name _____

Colour code _____

Nationality/Accent _____

Age – child ◯ teen ◯ adult ◯ elderly ◯

Gender – male ♂ female ♀ other ◯

Tempo – slow ◯ regular ◯ fast ◯

Pitch – low ◯ regular ◯ high ◯

Personality traits _____

_____

Character quirks _____

Other voice description _____

_____

Notes _____

_____

_____

Book title _____

Character name _____

Colour code _____

Nationality/Accent _____

Age – child ◯ teen ◯ adult ◯ elderly ◯

Gender – male ♂ female ♀ other ◯

Tempo – slow ◯ regular ◯ fast ◯

Pitch – low ◯ regular ◯ high ◯

Personality traits _____

_____

Character quirks _____

Other voice description _____

_____

Notes _____

_____

_____

Book title _____

Character name _____

Colour code _____

Nationality/Accent _____

Age – child ◯ teen ◯ adult ◯ elderly ◯

Gender – male ♂ female ♀ other ◯

Tempo – slow ◯ regular ◯ fast ◯

Pitch – low ◯ regular ◯ high ◯

Personality traits _____

_____

Character quirks _____

Other voice description _____

_____

Notes _____

_____

_____

Book title _____

Character name _____

Colour code _____

Nationality/Accent _____

Age – child ◯ teen ◯ adult ◯ elderly ◯

Gender – male ♂ female ♀ other ◯

Tempo – slow ◯ regular ◯ fast ◯

Pitch – low ◯ regular ◯ high ◯

Personality traits _____

_____

Character quirks _____

Other voice description _____

_____

Notes _____

_____

_____

Book title _____

Character name _____

Colour code _____

Nationality/Accent _____

Age – child ◯ teen ◯ adult ◯ elderly ◯

Gender – male ♂ female ♀ other ◯

Tempo – slow ◯ regular ◯ fast ◯

Pitch – low ◯ regular ◯ high ◯

Personality traits _____

_____

Character quirks _____

Other voice description _____

_____

Notes _____

_____

_____

Book title _____

Character name _____

Colour code _____

Nationality/Accent _____

Age – child ◯ teen ◯ adult ◯ elderly ◯

Gender – male ♂ female ♀ other ◯

Tempo – slow ◯ regular ◯ fast ◯

Pitch – low ◯ regular ◯ high ◯

Personality traits _____

_____

Character quirks _____

Other voice description _____

_____

Notes _____

_____

_____

Book title _____

Character name _____

Colour code _____

Nationality/Accent _____

Age – child ◯ teen ◯ adult ◯ elderly ◯

Gender – male ♂ female ♀ other ◯

Tempo – slow ◯ regular ◯ fast ◯

Pitch – low ◯ regular ◯ high ◯

Personality traits _____

_____

Character quirks _____

Other voice description _____

_____

Notes _____

_____

_____

Book title _____

Character name _____

Colour code _____

Nationality/Accent _____

Age – child ◯ teen ◯ adult ◯ elderly ◯

Gender – male ♂ female ♀ other ◯

Tempo – slow ◯ regular ◯ fast ◯

Pitch – low ◯ regular ◯ high ◯

Personality traits _____

_____

Character quirks _____

Other voice description _____

_____

Notes _____

_____

_____

Book title _____

Character name _____

Colour code _____

Nationality/Accent _____

Age – child ◯ teen ◯ adult ◯ elderly ◯

Gender – male ♂ female ♀ other ◯

Tempo – slow ◯ regular ◯ fast ◯

Pitch – low ◯ regular ◯ high ◯

Personality traits _____

_____

Character quirks _____

Other voice description _____

_____

Notes _____

_____

_____

Book title _____

Character name _____

Colour code _____

Nationality/Accent _____

Age – child ◯ teen ◯ adult ◯ elderly ◯

Gender – male ♂ female ♀ other ◯

Tempo – slow ◯ regular ◯ fast ◯

Pitch – low ◯ regular ◯ high ◯

Personality traits _____

_____

Character quirks _____

Other voice description _____

_____

Notes _____

_____

_____

Book title _____

Character name _____

Colour code _____

Nationality/Accent _____

Age – child ◯ teen ◯ adult ◯ elderly ◯

Gender – male ♂ female ♀ other ◯

Tempo – slow ◯ regular ◯ fast ◯

Pitch – low ◯ regular ◯ high ◯

Personality traits _____

_____

Character quirks _____

Other voice description _____

_____

Notes _____

_____

_____

Book title _____

Character name _____

Colour code _____

Nationality/Accent _____

Age – child ◯ teen ◯ adult ◯ elderly ◯

Gender – male ♂ female ♀ other ◯

Tempo – slow ◯ regular ◯ fast ◯

Pitch – low ◯ regular ◯ high ◯

Personality traits _____

_____

Character quirks _____

Other voice description _____

_____

Notes _____

_____

_____

Book title _____

Character name _____

Colour code _____

Nationality/Accent _____

Age – child ○ teen ○ adult ○ elderly ○

Gender – male ♂ female ♀ other ○

Tempo – slow ○ regular ○ fast ○

Pitch – low ○ regular ○ high ○

Personality traits _____

_____

Character quirks _____

Other voice description _____

_____

Notes _____

_____

_____

Book title _____

Character name _____

Colour code _____

Nationality/Accent _____

Age – child ◯ teen ◯ adult ◯ elderly ◯

Gender – male ♂ female ♀ other ◯

Tempo – slow ◯ regular ◯ fast ◯

Pitch – low ◯ regular ◯ high ◯

Personality traits _____

_____

Character quirks _____

Other voice description _____

_____

Notes _____

_____

_____

Book title _____

Character name _____

Colour code _____

Nationality/Accent _____

Age – child ◯ teen ◯ adult ◯ elderly ◯

Gender – male ♂ female ♀ other ◯

Tempo – slow ◯ regular ◯ fast ◯

Pitch – low ◯ regular ◯ high ◯

Personality traits _____

_____

Character quirks _____

Other voice description _____

_____

Notes _____

_____

_____

Book title _____

Character name _____

Colour code _____

Nationality/Accent _____

Age – child ◯ teen ◯ adult ◯ elderly ◯

Gender – male ♂ female ♀ other ◯

Tempo – slow ◯ regular ◯ fast ◯

Pitch – low ◯ regular ◯ high ◯

Personality traits _____

_____

Character quirks _____

Other voice description _____

_____

Notes _____

_____

_____

Book title _____

Character name _____

Colour code _____

Nationality/Accent _____

Age – child ◯ teen ◯ adult ◯ elderly ◯

Gender – male ♂ female ♀ other ◯

Tempo – slow ◯ regular ◯ fast ◯

Pitch – low ◯ regular ◯ high ◯

Personality traits _____

_____

Character quirks _____

Other voice description _____

_____

Notes _____

_____

_____

Book title _____

Character name _____

Colour code _____

Nationality/Accent _____

Age – child ◯ teen ◯ adult ◯ elderly ◯

Gender – male ♂ female ♀ other ◯

Tempo – slow ◯ regular ◯ fast ◯

Pitch – low ◯ regular ◯ high ◯

Personality traits _____

_____

Character quirks _____

Other voice description _____

_____

Notes _____

_____

_____

Book title _____

Character name _____

Colour code _____

Nationality/Accent _____

Age – child ◯ teen ◯ adult ◯ elderly ◯

Gender – male ♂ female ♀ other ◯

Tempo – slow ◯ regular ◯ fast ◯

Pitch – low ◯ regular ◯ high ◯

Personality traits _____

_____

Character quirks _____

Other voice description _____

_____

Notes _____

_____

_____

Book title _____

Character name _____

Colour code _____

Nationality/Accent _____

Age – child ◯ teen ◯ adult ◯ elderly ◯

Gender – male ♂ female ♀ other ◯

Tempo – slow ◯ regular ◯ fast ◯

Pitch – low ◯ regular ◯ high ◯

Personality traits _____

_____

Character quirks _____

Other voice description _____

_____

Notes _____

_____

_____

Book title _____

Character name _____

Colour code _____

Nationality/Accent _____

Age – child ◯ teen ◯ adult ◯ elderly ◯

Gender – male ♂ female ♀ other ◯

Tempo – slow ◯ regular ◯ fast ◯

Pitch –   low ◯ regular ◯ high ◯

Personality traits _____

_____

Character quirks _____

Other voice description _____

_____

Notes _____

_____

_____

Book title _____

Character name _____

Colour code _____

Nationality/Accent _____

Age – child ◯ teen ◯ adult ◯ elderly ◯

Gender – male ♂ female ♀ other ◯

Tempo – slow ◯ regular ◯ fast ◯

Pitch – low ◯ regular ◯ high ◯

Personality traits _____

_____

Character quirks _____

Other voice description _____

_____

Notes _____

_____

_____

Book title _____

Character name _____

Colour code _____

Nationality/Accent _____

Age – child ◯ teen ◯ adult ◯ elderly ◯

Gender – male ♂ female ♀ other ◯

Tempo – slow ◯ regular ◯ fast ◯

Pitch – low ◯ regular ◯ high ◯

Personality traits _____

_____

Character quirks _____

Other voice description _____

_____

Notes _____

_____

_____

Book title _____

Character name _____

Colour code _____

Nationality/Accent _____

Age – child ◯ teen ◯ adult ◯ elderly ◯

Gender – male ♂ female ♀ other ◯

Tempo – slow ◯ regular ◯ fast ◯

Pitch – low ◯ regular ◯ high ◯

Personality traits _____

_____

Character quirks _____

Other voice description _____

_____

Notes _____

_____

_____

Book title _____

Character name _____

Colour code _____

Nationality/Accent _____

Age – child ◯ teen ◯ adult ◯ elderly ◯

Gender – male ♂ female ♀ other ◯

Tempo – slow ◯ regular ◯ fast ◯

Pitch – low ◯ regular ◯ high ◯

Personality traits _____

_____

Character quirks _____

Other voice description _____

_____

Notes _____

_____

_____

Book title _____

Character name _____

Colour code _____

Nationality/Accent _____

Age – child ◯ teen ◯ adult ◯ elderly ◯

Gender – male ♂ female ♀ other ◯

Tempo – slow ◯ regular ◯ fast ◯

Pitch – low ◯ regular ◯ high ◯

Personality traits _____

_____

Character quirks _____

Other voice description _____

_____

Notes _____

_____

_____

Book title _____

Character name _____

Colour code _____

Nationality/Accent _____

Age – child ◯ teen ◯ adult ◯ elderly ◯

Gender – male ♂ female ♀ other ◯

Tempo – slow ◯ regular ◯ fast ◯

Pitch – low ◯ regular ◯ high ◯

Personality traits _____

_____

Character quirks _____

Other voice description _____

_____

Notes _____

_____

_____

Book title _____

Character name _____

Colour code _____

Nationality/Accent _____

Age – child ◯ teen ◯ adult ◯ elderly ◯

Gender – male ♂ female ♀ other ◯

Tempo – slow ◯ regular ◯ fast ◯

Pitch – low ◯ regular ◯ high ◯

Personality traits _____

_____

Character quirks _____

Other voice description _____

_____

Notes _____

_____

_____

Book title _____

Character name _____

Colour code _____

Nationality/Accent _____

Age – child ◯ teen ◯ adult ◯ elderly ◯

Gender – male ♂ female ♀ other ◯

Tempo – slow ◯ regular ◯ fast ◯

Pitch – low ◯ regular ◯ high ◯

Personality traits _____

_____

Character quirks _____

Other voice description _____

_____

Notes _____

_____

_____

Book title _____

Character name _____

Colour code _____

Nationality/Accent _____

Age – child ◯ teen ◯ adult ◯ elderly ◯

Gender – male ♂ female ♀ other ◯

Tempo – slow ◯ regular ◯ fast ◯

Pitch – low ◯ regular ◯ high ◯

Personality traits _____

_____

Character quirks _____

Other voice description _____

_____

Notes _____

_____

_____

Book title _____

Character name _____

Colour code _____

Nationality/Accent _____

Age – child ◯ teen ◯ adult ◯ elderly ◯

Gender – male ♂ female ♀ other ◯

Tempo – slow ◯ regular ◯ fast ◯

Pitch – low ◯ regular ◯ high ◯

Personality traits _____

_____

Character quirks _____

Other voice description _____

_____

Notes _____

_____

_____

Book title _____

Character name _____

Colour code _____

Nationality/Accent _____

Age – child ◯ teen ◯ adult ◯ elderly ◯

Gender – male ♂ female ♀ other ◯

Tempo – slow ◯ regular ◯ fast ◯

Pitch – low ◯ regular ◯ high ◯

Personality traits _____

_____

Character quirks _____

Other voice description _____

_____

Notes _____

_____

_____

Book title _____

Character name _____

Colour code _____

Nationality/Accent _____

Age – child ◯ teen ◯ adult ◯ elderly ◯

Gender – male ♂ female ♀ other ◯

Tempo – slow ◯ regular ◯ fast ◯

Pitch – low ◯ regular ◯ high ◯

Personality traits _____

_____

Character quirks _____

Other voice description _____

_____

Notes _____

_____

_____

Book title _____

Character name _____

Colour code _____

Nationality/Accent _____

Age – child ◯ teen ◯ adult ◯ elderly ◯

Gender – male ♂ female ♀ other ◯

Tempo – slow ◯ regular ◯ fast ◯

Pitch – low ◯ regular ◯ high ◯

Personality traits _____

_____

Character quirks _____

Other voice description _____

_____

Notes _____

_____

_____

Book title _____

Character name _____

Colour code _____

Nationality/Accent _____

Age – child ◯ teen ◯ adult ◯ elderly ◯

Gender – male ♂ female ♀ other ◯

Tempo – slow ◯ regular ◯ fast ◯

Pitch – low ◯ regular ◯ high ◯

Personality traits _____

_____

Character quirks _____

Other voice description _____

_____

Notes _____

_____

_____

Book title _____

Character name _____

Colour code _____

Nationality/Accent _____

Age – child ◯ teen ◯ adult ◯ elderly ◯

Gender – male ♂ female ♀ other ◯

Tempo – slow ◯ regular ◯ fast ◯

Pitch – low ◯ regular ◯ high ◯

Personality traits _____

_____

Character quirks _____

Other voice description _____

_____

Notes _____

_____

_____

Book title _____

Character name _____

Colour code _____

Nationality/Accent _____

Age – child ◯ teen ◯ adult ◯ elderly ◯

Gender – male ♂ female ♀ other ◯

Tempo – slow ◯ regular ◯ fast ◯

Pitch – low ◯ regular ◯ high ◯

Personality traits _____

_____

Character quirks _____

Other voice description _____

_____

Notes _____

_____

_____

Book title _____

Character name _____

Colour code _____

Nationality/Accent _____

Age – child ◯ teen ◯ adult ◯ elderly ◯

Gender – male ♂ female ♀ other ◯

Tempo – slow ◯ regular ◯ fast ◯

Pitch – low ◯ regular ◯ high ◯

Personality traits _____

_____

Character quirks _____

Other voice description _____

_____

Notes _____

_____

_____

Book title _____

Character name _____

Colour code _____

Nationality/Accent _____

Age – child ◯ teen ◯ adult ◯ elderly ◯

Gender – male ♂ female ♀ other ◯

Tempo – slow ◯ regular ◯ fast ◯

Pitch – low ◯ regular ◯ high ◯

Personality traits _____

_____

Character quirks _____

Other voice description _____

_____

Notes _____

_____

_____

Book title _____